lost

and

certain

of it

other works by

Bryce Milligan

poetry

Daysleepers & Other Poems (1984)
Litany Sung at Hell's Gate (1990)
From Inside the Tree (1990)
Working the Stone (1993)
Alms for Oblivion: A Poem in Seven Parts (2003)

young adult fiction

Battle of the Alamo (1990, 1999)
Comanche Captive (1990, 2005)
Lawmen: Stories of Men Who Tamed the West (1994)
With the Wind, Kevin Dolan (1987)
Kevin Dolan (German ed., 1994)

children's books

Brigid's Cloak: An Ancient Irish Story (2002)
*The Prince of Ireland
and the Three Magic Stallions* (2003)

books edited

¡Floricanto Sí! A Collection of Latina Poetry (1998)
*Daughters of the Fifth Sun: A Collection of Latina
Fiction and Poetry* (1995)

LOST

and certain of it

Bryce Milligan

D'Amor no'm puosc partir, c'Amors mi pren,
E qan m'en cuich emblar plus mi repren
Ab un esgart don mos cors s'escompren,
Qe m fai venir de lieis en cui m'empren.

– Aimeric de Peguilhan
Languedoc, ca. 1205

London
2006

First printing

ISBN: 1899179992

Aark Arts
Sudeep Sen, Publisher
65 Greenford Road
Harrow HA1 3QF • London, England
(www.sudeepsen.com)
This title also distributed in the U.S.
by Wings Press (www.wingspress.com)
and Small Press Distribution
(www.spdbooks.org)

Photo by the author, taken
in the woods behind Robert Frost's
farm in Derry, New Hampshire.
Illustration on page 27 from
an etching by the author.

Contents

Acknowledgments

"Lost and certain of it" first appeared in *Working the Stone* (Wings, 1993).

"Instructions for the funeral" first appeared in *TEX!* (Dallas: The Writers Garret, 1998). Recipient of the *"Tex!* poetry prize;" contest judged by Rita Dove.

"Summers in the country" and "His last pocketknife" first appeared in *The Texas Observer*. "Summers in the country" was included in *Is This Forever, or What? Poems and Paintings from Texas,* edited by Naomi Shihab Nye (Green- willow / HarperCollins, 2003).

"Trying not to fall," "The silence inside the city," and "Wild mustard" were published in "This Week in Jazz ..." (San Antonio Jazz Network's e-newsletter – http://www.mandalamusic.com) "Jazz Poetry" section, a regular feature.

"Black Hair" was a finalist in the 2002 Kerrville Folk Festival New Folks Songwriting Contest.

"Monuments," "Trying not to fall," "Instructions for the funeral," "She sets the pace,"and "Between one crack and another" were published in the California-based web lit mag, *Tertulia,* http://www.tertuliamagazine.com), February 2004, along with a lengthy interview (featured poet for this issue).

"Monuments" appeared in *Windhover* (2005).

Many thanks to Sudeep Sen for choosing to include my work in his Contemporary World Poetry Series from Aark Arts, and for allowing this poet to have so much input in the design of his books. It is a distinct honor to be numbered among Sudeep's poets. Thanks also to Roberto Bonazzi for proofing and for his sage editorial eye, not to mention the good conversations, and to Donald Hall, who commented on several early drafts of these poems. Hope I eliminated all the dead metaphors, Don. Special thanks to my wife, Mary, for all her love and support, and for putting up with this strange life I live. And as always, thanks to Cerddwen, Inanna, and their cohorts, be they celestial or earthly.

FOREWORD

The first work by Bryce Milligan I read was *Working the Stone* in the mid-1990s. I was moved then by the lyricism of his language and his honesty of stance. Subsequently, I have read more of his work, heard him read his poetry, heard him sing songs he has written, and heard him play musical instruments – Milligan is a true 'bard' poet in the best sense of the word.

In 2003, I published Milligan's *Alms for Oblivion* as part of the Aark Arts 'Contemporary World Poetry' Series I edit. This long poem in seven parts is like a medieval Rajasthani miniature painting – Miltonic in ambition and expanse, yet understated and image-packed like a Japanese haiku. It is an oratorical tour de force – haunting, cadenced, mythic, and lyrical. This is a classic 'quest poem' where the muse-poet abandons everything – intellect, practicality, passion – only to lose himself in the very same things, things that are the ultimate essentials of artistic breathing, creation, and life. Orchestral in scope and shape, Milligan's *Alms for Oblivion* is a little gem of an epic.

Lost and Certain of It is a collection of his newer poems and songs. The title poem, however, first appeared in *Working the Stone*, and the others in various magazines, journals and anthologies. The new work is simultaneously personal and universal, as well as lyrical and imagistic. Many poems are dedicated to fellow artists and friends – an aspect that is worth noting because Milligan's own work functions as a crossover between poetry, music and art where the word, phrase, line, and idea on the page meet the highly practised tenor of orality and vocal modulation.

It is for this reason that I am glad that Milligan has chosen to publish his songs (that appear as the second section of this book), as this juxtaposes his more pure poetry along with lyric writing. This gives a true picture of him as a poet and artist – displaying his skill with words that are not only meant to be read quietly but also to be read out loud, and the song compositions sung aloud.

True reading aloud of poetry is an important and ancient tradition that often gets lost in the modern world of brazen sound-bite driven 'performance poetry'. Too often what might sound acceptable on stage, when read privately by an unbiased reader, falls flat on the page because the writing quality is poorer than the quality of speech delivery and does not stand up to the fanfare the performer poet might create on stage. Bryce Milligan's works transcend these limitations and coalesce many traditions and genres beautifully. *Lost and Certain of It* is a book to rejoice in and savour.

– Sudeep Sen
author of *Postmarked India: New & Selected Poems* (HarperCollins)

November 2005
New Delhi & London

LOST

and certain of it

A Short Note

I am often asked which of my many hats I prefer –
poet, songwriter, children's author, novelist, book
designer, anthologist, critic, publisher, teacher, maker
of guitars and drums and dulcimers, musician. . . . The
truth is, they are all manifestations of a creative life
that seeks simply to serve the muse. And this is why I
have here, as in the past, included some songs with a
collection of poems. To my mind, there is little differ-
ence between the two forms except that songs are more
tolerant of what contemporary poets and critics would
deem topical and cultural clichés. So be it, though I
would hazard that as often as not what appears to be a
"love song" is really a hymn to the persons, things and
ideas that inspire us to create, no matter what the end
product.

Rhythmic structures and regular rhyme schemes
are certainly more obvious in songs, but they are no less
controlled in these poems than they are in the songs. To
me, the craft is as important as the topic – it is the mak-
ing that matters. Sir Philip Sidney once wrote: "Fool,
said my muse to me, look in thy heart and write."
Indeed, that *is* the command, although she could have
added "well" to the sentence. Perhaps it was implicit.
As Dante's favorite troubador, Aimeric de Peguilhan,
described it, one look from the muse "consumes the
heart, inflames [the poet]." Of course, the heat of the
fire depends upon the quality of the fuel. I shall now go
dabble with wood for a while and leave the words to
defend themselves.

– B.M.

2

Lost and certain of it

Lost and certain of it, the woods crowd in
allowing only glimpses of the track
that was so clear and broad and well traveled

only moments back where the sun fell bright
between the leaves to dapple the mast, but
lost and certain of it, the woods crowd in

spinning the senses like leaves in a wind
risen from the past to obscure the path
that was so clear and broad and well traveled.

A broad green stream appears for a moment
strewn with rippled light and autumn's soft flames.
Lost and certain of it, the woods crowd in

and the stream slips away into the deeper shade,
taking with it the desire for the path
that was so clear and broad and well traveled,

taking with it the memory of the last
dregs of love and I am glad that I am
lost and certain of it.
                            Let the woods crowd out
all that is clear and broad and well traveled.

Summers in the Country

for Tino Villanueva

Summers in the country, I was the city boy
up from Dallas to visit the farm, up to visit
up to explore up to no good up to corrupt (those
old ladies said behind their curtains) those
country girls those twelve-year-old cowgirls
who snuck beers behind the rodeo stands and
those boys who talked about which cows were
best who wondered what the hell I found so
interesting about the damn grave yard and
why did I always have a damn book with me
and was I writing down notes to give their
damn mothers or what.
                              Summers in the country
I was Huckleberry looking for Jim and a river
I was Woody looking for a song and glory I was
Meg trying to tesser and Davy trying to trap
the perfect coon for the perfect hat and trying
to get it all down on a backpocket steno pad
taking shorthand on life and getting curiouser
and curiouser about how my parents survived
this damn town at all.
                              Summers in the country
I drove grandpa's air conditioned tractor
while field hands bent double down the long rows
sometimes singing chopping cotton always sweating
everyone of them a philosopher of labor
a poet of the machete an Odysseus
making his way back home every one of them
knowing more about the land than I ever would
in a lifetime of summers in the country.

4

Wild mustard

for Mance

Sudden sunlight steams the wild mustard,
heavy headed with the vanishing mist,
and for miles the scent makes the sodden heat
worth enduring: windows down, elbow slung
against the warm damp wind.

All along this southern highway clouds
rise out of the ground to surround treetop
islands, each mysterious just so long
as it takes the gray incensed fog to fade
into the yellow light.

One hot May morning thirty years gone
I walked these Navasota bottomlands
with old man Lipscomb: "I's up way early
for a bluesman," and he laughed at the sun.
We stood in that rich light

until Mama's sausage and biscuits
drew us inside to a day of stories
and guitar licks I would never get right –
not even understand until I smelled
wild mustard in your hair.

The silence inside the city

I wait for sleep
like some late bus
with the A/C
vents screwed tight
and the windows
opened wide to the night
to the blatant moon
filled like an autumn pie
with memories –
when the jazz begins
to cut through the traffic,
floating out from
the neon-drenched cafes
and acid-thin guitar licks
sizzle down from some radio
and some woman's talking
too loud to God
while a dumpster lid
screeches open
and shut
open and
shut
and all I can hear
is me thinking
of you

Where were you

Where were you when
the pecans fell and
I crawled all afternoon
alone among the mast

to gather this late harvest
together with the old tomcat
who lay sunning himself
missing your rare touch

I wanted you when
the shattered shells were
scattered across the news-
papers on our oldest table

Where were you when
the fall winds rattled
sash on sill and whistled
shrill as the memories

that rise with the
autumn aroma
of these southern pies

7

Trying not to fall

for Joy Harjo

There is a woman with a saxophone
blowing the blues out of time
raising tones like thunderheads
and tones like lightning,
tones like the gray mist
rising on an Oklahoma river.

There is a woman with a saxophone,
golden horn handed down
one prophet to another
one shaman to the next
beginning as a scrannel flute
golden reed from the Chattahoochee
drawn at dawn and cured inside
a medicine bundle somewhere
in America, somewhere
in time
flint carved its first song,
the song of awakening
after long sleep, after death.

There is a woman with a saxophone
breathing in the same air
drawn through the sacred stem
when no white hand had laid claim
or shed blood anywhere
in America.

There is a woman with a saxophone,
woman of wind and water
blowing the blues out of time
woman with hair like the raven
that hangs in the sky calling the future
as he sees it, hair blue
blue as blackbird wings in sunshine
with eyes like black holes
in time, ends and beginnings
quick as grace notes.

There is a woman with a saxophone
on the banks of the Muscogee
rising into the cloud of her music
rising like sacred smoke
rising like stomp dance bonfire flames
rising like warriors bound
for the long paths of the milky way.
There is a woman with a saxophone
trying
not to fall.

Five Years Gone

for Jane Kenyon

Behind the house, Jane's garden is overgrown;
between there and Eagle Pond only ghosts:
trains that run silent over the grade's gray stones
littered with rusted steel spikes, heavy bolts.

Beside the lake, a favored spot, good for sun,
good for water, only slightly wilder than
Jane's garden where her spring ministrations
kept the volunteer maples down, so eager
to see the seasons in and out, in and out.

Down the road a mile there is a stone where
anonymous hands swap scraps of poetry
and sea shells for pine cones, single ear rings
or other scraps of poetry, some of it
Jane's, mostly not, some taking, some giving.
Just over the fence, a small apple tree drops
the sweetest fruit I have ever tasted.

His last pocketknife

Granddaddy honed his pocketknives
until their blades were slivered winter moons,
black-backed silver crescents, razors but

useless in the end, too fragile to carve.
Old ones were retired to a cigar box
beside his bed where they lay with his pipes,

the blackened briars that killed him.
He clutched a new knife with dead
pallid fingers when we found him,

chair rocked to the wall, his hourglass
whetstone shattered on the porch,
the black shards so thin

they resembled the tea leaves in a bone
china cup. All my life since I have honed
his last pocketknife against too-soft stones.

Visiting the Painter Lady:
Canyon, Texas, 1917

Once a week for six weeks, while farmboys died in France
Pauline visited Georgia – packed up her precious paints,
her half-finished flower scenes, cranked up the Model T
and rattled down the rutted wagon track that led
away west to the newly grated gravel road,

gearing down and down toward the top of the one long hill,
pausing there to catch a breath of wind and pretend
for a moment that the scent of scrub cedar was sweet pine,
then sailing the other side in neutral, fast enough to skim
the sometime-quicksand crust of the Canadian River ford.

Pauline spent an hour with the painter lady at the College,
two neat brick buildings overlooking Palo Duro Canyon,
that sudden red rift across tawny plains so stark
as to inspire imagination in a fence post, just to fill in
the colossal emptiness. Pauline painted scenes

of mountain meadows she had never seen, portraits
of unborn daughters in starched pinafores,
a woman in a grass skirt with a ukulele. Georgia
shaped colors: rich red rifts across tawny dreams
beneath looming orchid skies.

Reading Victoria's Secrets

I. 1991

I'll never know what Victoria wears
beneath these vintage dresses,
granny calicos hugging slim hips
no granny ever had, with
lacy necklines that dip too deep
into my too macho imagination.

Into this high school classroom
she strolls hipper than I
recall any hippies of twenty
years back, her black eyes
determined to tap
her own rhythms

though she fears they
may be echoes only.
Here they come, I think,
the poems of young ennui
of love and suffering
and sure enough

I have Victoria's secrets
open before me, laid out
like polished river stones
each with a history.
My desk strewn with desires
and questions and power,

I carefully select the blue pencil.

II. 1993

Into my college comp she strolls
with a sheaf of poems beneath
her arm like an immigrant
with her papers, proof of the right
to be where no one should question
her right to be.
                    Cat like,
ready to pounce or run
weep or scream,
equally confused and confusing.
She has put her power somewhere
she cannot reach. It is growing
and cannot be edited.
                    She will
marry the bastard and vanish,
leaving unfinished papers
and poems smoldering
like coals in my hands.

14

III. 1995

He beat her. The bastard
raised his fist and hammered
his frustrations home at home,
claimed that he was the poet,
not she.

Then Victoria took this secret
and wrung poetry from it like
strong women have always wrung
sex out of linens
beside thousands of streams
for thousands of years
in the sight of the whole village.

Victoria stood up in her black and silver,
took to the microphone
and dripped that man out of her soul
one word at a time, out of her body
until all the machismo infection
was drained away.

I know what Victoria is like
beneath those vintage dresses:
made and maker,
granite block and steel chisel,
muse and mother,
seething with secrets within
secrets within secrets.

Instructions for the funeral

Find the right hill
the highest, rockiest
in this too flat land,
that one north of town
with no roads, no paths
but water tracks

Do your best to avoid
the law; follow only
the oldest conventions;
especially avoid
any professionals
in the business of death

Cut no living wood
but seek out the scrub
cedar brush blown down
and weave a lattice couch,
cover it with the old
four-stripe Hudson Bay

Lay me out in the morning
in my oldest jeans
and the red Guatemalan shirt
with buffalo nickel buttons
to provide the crows
with whatnots

Monuments:

the things that remain
to remind us of what we were
before we were without that
which prompts us to remember,
but here the monument is a thing
of air, a column like Jehovah
in the Sinai, first flame then nothing
but smoke, dust and smoke.

The monument
in the mind is an emptiness
in the air where once
was flesh and blood,
concrete and steel,
but only the emptiness
in the mind remains.

The children gathered
in this classroom have built
the only monument that will remain,
burnt it into their futures
to keep as we have always kept
the deaths of kings and presidents,
astronauts and princesses,
and old men making salt
by the sea:
              "Where were you when . . . ?"
              "What were you wearing . . . ?"

Steel is always simply steel,
subject to the slow fires of rust,
but this monument of smoke
remains, terrible
as Jehovah in the desert.

Water's Rising

water's rising, and you who were caught
in last year's flood, you are ready to scramble
onto the roof of the car and scream

but on this lonely backstreet, with a good
meal still warm in my belly and the wine
still sweet in my mouth, there are no lights

there is no cell phone, no traffic
no friendly strangers out for a stroll —
there is only the dark, and the current

Revising a story among wolves

He stands just beyond the reach
of the brilliance that transects
the heart of the forest,
coat deckled with green sun and gray
shadows – adequate camouflage
if he does not bare his teeth
or let the light catch his eyes.

I loiter on the path, sniffing
columbines, a lupine Ferdinand
struggling to contain the strength
that boils in my shoulders and loins
waiting for the storied red cape
to come skipping down this
ancient path.

His eyes glint, yellow and black.
"Get ready," he says. "She's coming."
"How do you know?"
"I have never known her not to."

When she does appear
she is older than I expected,
experienced perhaps, I think,
in the ways of my kind,
human or lupine,
and I feel my hunger, the old
gnawing in my belly,
slide lower, burning
darker and stronger
than the honorable desire
for a morsel of flesh.

19

"Good morning," I say,
suave, confident
of the conversation's course.
This is the moment I was made for,
my tutor in the shadows
has told me, and again
I see his tongue slide over white
incisors, savoring
the flavors granted
only once in our lives.

"Where are you going to
and where have you been
on this fine morning?"

She responds without words,
drawing back the hood
staring boldly
brown eyes into black,
reaching out to scratch
behind my ears,
smoothing my coat,
fingers splayed in my fur,
reaching, reaching
beneath.

This is not the story
I was told, but the troubling
dream I could never deny.
Her small walnuts brush
against my wet nose.
Closing my eyes, I
willingly exchange
this moment
for all the meals of my life.

My companion howls
when he sees her draw
the silver knife,
but I do not flinch.
Her caress is worth
every inch
of bright steel
sliding into
my heart.

Between one crack and another

On this rock face, as on every other
there is a fine line, almost indecipherable
lying between courage and madness.
You discover it between one hand hold
and the next, between one loop of rope
and another, and you find it alone.

Faith in finger strength, in the assurance
of internal balance when all that matters
is down; faith in the ability to test
through wool and leather and steel
the stability of a two-inch ledge, itself
a product of ice and sunlight.

Faith in these is suddenly one with one's
faith in the ability to fly, to free fall
in full control, as if will alone could turn
splayed fingers into wing tips guiding
your hawk-body's slow descent, tying
time into Gordian conundrums.

Alone in this December rain, I watch
a sidewalk of bobbing umbrellas,
stare at the fine line between ascent
and free fall, fit my fingers into one crack
then another, sensing the difference
between talon and wing tip.

Lightning

The days that lack that flash:
heat on the horizon,
thunderheads painted bright
with the promise of rain

to wash the desert dust
from needle and flower,
yielding up red and yellow
explosions on each cactus' tower.

The days that lack that flash
bring me careening back
to your eyes that I cannot
tell from lightning.

Metaphor

I need a metaphor that will transform
this skeleton of passion into some
thing that breathes fire rather than the still air
of considered conundrums, into some
thing that stands of its own accord against
time and these chill unseasonable winds.

I need a shape-shifting incantation
to turn the shaman's cape into the shape
of the panther it contained, to take in
whole the one mind, the one soul that brought forth
the transforming morpheme, that piece of sound
that like some particle born of theory

remains unfound, unseen, but whose effects
attend all the invisible powers,
that force all our hours into vectors
pointing to new futures rather than past
cycles. I need a metaphor to change,
I need a metaphor, a master rune,

a word, a sign unspoken since time was
set in motion. *Deus erat verbum.*
I need to warp this, our reality,
to be the body that bends your body,
to create the pulsar, the double star.
I need a metaphor to change, to change.

Stone conundrums

From a certain angle
in the desert distance
out west of Nine Mile Draw
twin eroded mesas rise
like pubescent breasts.

The slopes sweep down
from the stone nipples to the scree
invisible from this one angle.
Only a few steps will bring
the rocky sprawl in sight and spoil

the memory with the reality
of stone detritus with its scorpions
and rattlesnakes and from there
my practical mind wanders
to hiking boots and fangs.

But I was describing the image
when accuracy got in the way
as it tends to do when all you want
is to lean into familiar dreams
of maybes and might-have-beens.

These twin desiccate landforms
describe the erosion of ten
thousand years' wind and,
from a single angle, one single
moment of eruptive life.

There is no hint of the under
curve to come – that precious
milky weight, made to bear life
against time and gravity, that would
draw me into this deadly scree.

She sets the pace

She sets the pace as I cannot,
does not allow the madness
of my momentary metaphor

to stay her steady progress,
will not bend when the winds shift
from lyric to narrative.

Rather she takes each step
as the marvel that it is,
standing as if at some scenic view

beside some mountain highway
absorbing each blue peak, each
snow-blotched pine while I,

impatient to see the next white pine
behind the next blue peak,
am always astounded

when she hands me the next line
polished and new
and fine.

Songs

Lady rides the rails in the
night-time, making music
as she rolls along.
Her guitar chimes in
iron-wheel time as
her life becomes
another song. She
is poetry, she is
fire, she is dreams
beyond desire: Grey
eyes gleaming in the
dusk, she leads them
to the place they must
decide what it is that sets
them free.

Lady Rides the Rails

(song)

Lady rides the rails in the night-time,
making music as she rolls along:
her guitar chimes in iron wheel time
as her life becomes another song.
She is poetry, she is fire,
she is dreams far beyond desire:
Grey eyes gleaming in the dusk
she leads us to the place we must
decide what it is that sets us free.

All along the Sunset Line
she leaves memories and melodies behind;
just like autumn's first cool breeze
in summer-dry leaves
she comforts the mind.

Lady takes the midnight train to New Orleans,
leaving Texas souls in the dust;
she leaves old men and young men wondering
what they'll do now their dreams have all gone bust.
She gave them poetry, she gave them fire,
she gave them dreams beyond their desires:
Grey eyes gleaming in the dusk
she led them to the place they must
decide what it was that set them free.

She's their power, she's their light,
she's white lace on a leather night,
she's the seventh note in a midnight blues,
she's the one you can't afford to lose.

On Bourbon Street the saxophones sing high –
hear 'em rip in rhythm with her hips;
and the poets sigh each time she walks by
and they pray to catch a word from her lips.
She gives them poetry, she gives them fire,
she gives them dreams hot off her wire:
Grey eyes gleaming in the dusk
she leads them to the place they must
decide what it is that sets them free –
decide what it is that sets them free –
decide what it is that makes them sing.

Black Hair

(song)

Late nights I wear your black hair close to my skin
after work is done, when dreaming begins.
I am younger then and you are my twin:
you still weave these sleepy spells.
There's not much I can do to change the world:
can't summon winds to make this sail unfurl.
I almost lost myself for one bright pearl;
now I'm filling up wishing wells.

This wasn't something that I planned to do –
The roadmap of your palm is lost in time.
But there's no choosing when it comes to you:
I have to keep loving you in rhyme.

Mornings find you still inside my mind:
and I wonder if you'll ever let me find
that little part of you that you left behind
that turned my world around.
Hopeless days of watching you go by –
I can't use confusion as an alibi –
so now this hawk dreams of an endless sky
with no need to come to ground.

This wasn't something that I planned to do –
The roadmap of your palm is lost in time.
But there's no choosing when it comes to you:
I have to keep loving you in rhyme.

Invisible crystals on a starry night,
ring the moon with echoed light:
whispered secrets like these just might
be what sets me free.
Still, I hear the siren songs that call
this midnight poet to brave that fall,
that make living on the edge seem all
that will let this dreaming be.

This wasn't something that I planned to do –
The roadmap of your palm is lost in time.
But there's no choosing when it comes to you:
I have to keep loving you in rhyme.

My Lady of the Woods

(song)

My lady of the woods
spins her spider-web stories:
catches hearts unawares;
catches dreams in her webs,
future poems and past glories,
songs like leaves in the air.

The wind carries ashes grey as her eyes.
My lady knows well she must fly.

My lady of the woods
brought me maples and cherries,
this dark mahogony air.
A willow dancer in the night:
white flame among embers
with the moonlight in her hair.

The wind carries ashes grey as her eyes.
My lady knows well she must fly.

My lady of the woods
wove me tunes for tomorrow
when she'll no longer be there.
These ashes I know well,
there's no doubt of the sorrow
with Lady Phoenix in the air.

These woods are no haven; take to the skies.
My lady knows well she must fly.

Look Who's Coming Now

(song for Dante and Beatrice)

He's sat beside the muse before,
watched all night outside her door,
he's waited for ten thousand dawns.
Ah, but look who's coming now.
Only once was she so close as now,
on a Florence street where he saw just how
time would wash over her like rain.
But he can't get that close again –
something about fire in the hand.

This time he thinks he'll get it right –
give up vices and follow the light
until he finds the other side of night
though hell might bar the way.
Only once was she so close as now,
on a Florence street where he saw just how
time would wash over her like rain.
But he can't get that close again –
something about fire in the hand.

He can't know what he's done
to deserve this second run
when he was so close to being done.

This time he says he'll get it straight
though there might be years to wait
before she opens that sacred gate
and welcomes him inside.
Only once was she so close as now,
on a Florence street where he saw just how
time would wash over her like rain.
But he just can't get that close again –
something about fire in the hand.

33

All My Texas Rivers

(song)

Goodbye to the Brazos,
Goodbye to the Red,
Goodbye to the mighty Rio Grande.
I'm headed west to higher ground
to where she laid her head,
but I'm traveling with my heart in my hand.

Goodbye to the Frio,
to the Llanos, East and West,
to the San Antonio's limpid greens and blues.
I'm leaving all the rivers,
springs and creeks I love the best
to do what my heart tells me I must do.

All my Texas rivers shimmer
pale as midnight ghosts,
and memories like arroyos run
from childhood to the coast.
But there's a line you cross sometimes,
like the Great Divide,
when life runs down
the shadowed side of hope.

Goodbye to you, old Trinity
and to little Bachman Creek,
to the Colorado and sparkling Barton Springs,
and to the Guadalupe's laughter
and the Limpia, oh so sweet,
I'll not forget the way your waters sing.

Goodbye my Canadian
with your sad Comanche tale.
Goodbye to the Pecos and Sabine.
She calls me like the sirens called
Ulysses as he sailed ...
and I hear all too clearly what she sings.

All my Texas rivers shimmer
pale as midnight ghosts,
and memories like arroyos run
from childhood to the coast.
But there's a line you cross sometimes,
like the Great Divide,
when life runs down
the shadowed side of hope.

Dark Freight

(song)

Once more I find
iron wheels in the night time –
I thought that was
a long gone fate.
But here I stand
like my grandfathers before me
waiting to jump
a west-bound freight.

Here she comes rumbling out of the moonrise,
to catch her you've got to run fast:
throw yourself through the doorway to paradise
and let the wheels of fate run freely at last.

How many times must
this circle be broken?
How many times can
a life go 'round?
When she comes she comes
 like some force of nature.
When she leaves she leaves
barren ground.

Here she comes rumbling out of the moonrise,
to catch her you've got to run fast:
throw yourself through the doorway to paradise
and let the wheels of fate run freely at last.

There're so many questions
I have wanted to ask you,
all my life and now
the time has come:
In this dark season
are these deaths without reason,
or do they come to some
cosmic sum?

Here she comes rumbling out of the moonrise,
to catch her you've got to run fast:
throw yourself through the doorway to paradise
and let the wheels of fate run freely at last.

Once more I find
a dark freight on the dream-line –
pulling away full of
damaged souls.
No more questions,
and no more answers;
nothing to do but to
let her roll.

Here she comes rumbling out of the moonrise,
to catch her you've got to run fast:
throw yourself through the doorway to paradise
and let the wheels of fate run freely at last.

AARK ARTS

PUBLISHERS OF FINE LITERATURE & THE ARTS

Authors, translators & artists
current & forthcoming:

Sachchidananda Vatsyayan
AGYEYA
Chidi AMAECHI
Zoran ANCHEVSKI
Wendy BARKER
Carlos BEDOYA
Charles BERNSTEIN
Michela BORZAGA
Fatim BOUTROS
Claudia BUDKE
Angus CALDER
Radha CHAKRAVARTY
Amit CHAUDHURI
Dilip CHITRE
Jibanananda DAS
Kwame DAWES
John F DEANE
Mahasweta DEVI
Karina MAGDALENA DORN
Tishani DOSHI
Timothy DOYLE
Marie-Cathrin GUERDAN
Kaiser HAQ
Andrea HAUSLER
Raul JAIME
Bernadette
SEONG-HAE JUNG

Adil JUSSAWALLA
Frauke LENGERMANN
Kelley LYNCH
MAHMUD
Leeya MEHTA
Hoshang MERCHANT
Bryce MILLIGAN
Kim MORRISSEY
Amir OR
Renate PAPKE
Aminur RAHMAN
Shamsur RAHMAN
R Raj RAO
Tomaz SALAMUN
Leela SAMSON
Fiona SAMPSON
Bina SARKAR
Sudeep SEN
Fazal SHAHABUDDIN
Mahendra SOLANKI
Rabindranath TAGORE
TANVIR
Jeet THAYIL
Stephen WATTS
John WELCH
John Hartley WILLIAMS
Avraham Ben YITSHAK

About the Author

Bryce Milligan is a modern troubadour, or, as Edward Hirsch called him recently, "a contemporary muse poet." *Bloomsbury Review* called him a "literary wizard." He calls himself a jack-of-all-genres, and it is true: he is a prolific poet, playwright, critic, novelist (for young adults) and children's author. Novelist and writing guru John Gardner wrote of Milligan's first book, *Daysleepers & Other Poems*, over twenty years ago: "Milligan is a real poet, with the real poet's sure voice, richness and variety, technical skill, and above all, delight in risk. . . . He pulls out all the stops, and because he knows so surely what he's talking about, and has an ear so unerring and an eye so partisan yet unblinking, he gets away with it. Reading him is a joy." Or as Daisy Aldan put it: "Here is an ancient intuitive vision and unity brought to the modern experience. This is a poet who will delight those who revere the word."

Milligan is also a musician and songwriter, a maker of guitars and other stringed instruments, an occasional sculptor, a teacher when he has to be, and an arts activist and organizer. Among other things he was a co-founder and long-time director of the Inter-American Bookfair, the Latina Letters annual conference, and two literary magazines. He is currently the publisher/editor of Wings Press in San Antonio, Texas. He has been married for 32 years to Mary, a librarian and sometime co-editor. They have two children, accomplished scholars both.

In *Something About the Author*, Milligan wrote: "Literature and writing are a great part of my life, but they are not everything. Creativity and craft are crucial, especially as they concern the idea of 'making.' Not much that is good in life just happens by accident. One makes a family, makes a song or poem, makes a book, makes a guitar, makes a garden, one even makes an old house continue to keep out the rain. This is why writers do not retire – to stop making is to stop being."

COLOPHON

Lost and Certain of It, by Bryce Milligan, has been printed on 60 pound non-acidic Fraser "Magna Carta Parchment" paper, containing 30 percent post consumer materials, and hand-bound. Titles have been set in Cochin Type. The text has been set in a contemporary version of Classic Bodoni. *Lost and Certain of It* was designed for Aark Arts at Gutenberg's Folly. The publisher and editor of Aark Arts is Sudeep Sen.

65 Greenford Road
Harrow HA1 3QF • London, England